2015

"We" Society
Poetry Anthology

www.printablereality.com

Copyright © 2015

Each author and/or poet asserts his or her own moral right to be identified as the author of his or her work(s).

ISBN 978-0-473-32197-0

All rights reserved. With the exception of short excerpts quoted for review purposes, no part of this book may be reproduced, stored in a retrieval system or transmitted in any form or by any electronic or mechanical means including photocopying, recording, information storage and retrieval systems, or otherwise, without prior permission in writing from the publisher.

The views of the poets included in this anthology are not necessarily those of the publisher, the judges, or the editors, who are not responsible for the accuracy of any statement contained herein. Each poet certifies that their work contained in this book is original and their own work. Each poet reserves the right to publish elsewhere their own work, as included in this book, if they so desire.

To order copies of this book please email gus@printablereality.com
or visit www.printablereality.com

Published by Printable Reality as a part of "Stage2Page" Series

Book design and layout: Geum Hye Kim and gus Simonovic

Special Thanks to all poets and:

Geum Hye Kim

John McDonald – SPLICE

Sally Legg – Te Henga Studios

Dr Jack Ross – Masey University

Yelena Dumanovic, Leslie Brennan & Gus Simonovic – Printable Reality

How it all started ?
With a poem:

TRUST

Its a such a lovely room …. spacious, open, welcoming.
The walls have been removed ….. barriers gone.

There was a living room here … and three bedrooms
and then …. another country beside it …. and another …. and another
you can tell by those marks on the ceiling, by lines on the floor.
Thats where the borders were in the past.

And now its one large room, a sweep
green and blue …   and the only lines are - shadows of the clouds
 … space to walk, space to sleep, space to love, space to grow, space to dance, space to trust, space to space out.

We finally brought the walls down!
All of them!!!
Less brick, more family … less enclosure, more bond
less borders, more playgrounds
less force, more security …. less secrets, more service.

Everybody has its own corner now, in this round space
and we can all be ….. … … in those corners
alone and together … together and alone
hungry for a living truth in human relationships.

Trust … trust … trust in betterment … trust in butterflies
trust in tension. …the TRUST

not in one self … not in the other

trust, not a compromise …. not a negotiation
trust, not a belief … not a surrender

Trust in harmony that is being created
 … trust in freedom …. trust in change
trust in finding and feeding the supreme sense of fulfillment.

TRUST is a new LOVE …
I trust you ! I trust you I trust you …

Gus Simonovic 2015

This anthology is a result of a project run by Printable Reality, Splice and Te Henga Studios.

An invitation was sent, at the beginning of 2015, for poets to express and share their thoughts and feelings on the topic of: - Society:

Language, and poetry in particular, is a mirror of our world. It captures and reflects some of the deepest human emotions. Language is one of our most highly evolved functions, a tool that we continue to reinvent, sharpen and expand. And, since language is designed entirely around our constantly evolving needs of expression, it is one way to both examine human life and ultimately connect with ourselves. Does poetry emerge from the need to express yourself? For a poet's words to be heard, published, quoted or sung? For their name to be remembered and cherished (one could say a perfect example of "me" society)? Or, as Eliot says: "Poetry is not an expression of personality, but an escape from personality"?

Either way, poetry created is for everybody. Poetry takes on another life when it is shared in authentic and intimate ways: through reading or listening. Is poetry reminding us about the "we" of society, that is about relationships, collaboration and cooperation? "

> 'We" society?
> It scares me to see
> how 'me' is our society.
> Or is it only me? "

How would you define the society we live in? Is it predominantly a common-good society, or an individualist society? Which society would you like to live in? What are we gaining and what are we losing as our culture changes? Can and does poetry enable us to explore and reflect on our values? How do language, communication and intention, belonging, dreams, aspirations and connection relate to the changing nature of the way we live and our values? How does poetry respond to what makes us human and what it means to belong to one another?

Table of Contents

Shortlisted poems are marked with *

10 in a packet* - Heather McQuillan --------------- 4

A Picture Paints Words - Tracey Peterson --------- 4

A Tool - E Wen Wong ------------------------------ 5

Accent - Sigred Yamit ---------------------------- 6

Amnesia - Janet Newman --------------------------- 7

Amsterdam - Jeni Curtis -------------------------- 8

Anthropology of Simia - Geum Hye Kim ------------ 9

At the Bay - Gill Ward --------------------------- 10

Caring* - Maris O'Rourke ------------------------- 12

Confessions - Steve McNeil ----------------------- 12

Date Night - Keith Nunes ------------------------- 14

Digital Natives - Anna Forsyth ------------------- 14

Engaging with Goya - Dorothy Howie --------------- 15

Enlightenment - Beverly Martens ------------------ 17

Enough - Vanessa Rare ---------------------------- 18

Everything about us* - Jane Williams ------------- 19

Farm* - Wes Lee ---------------------------------- 20

Fish of the sun - Peter Le Baige ----------------- 21

From me in Vanilla* - Kerrin P. Sharpe ----------- 22

Glittering Towers - Anastasia Cook --------------- 22

Haiku x 3 - Steven Clarkson ---------------------- 24

Heirlooms less abundant - Janean Cherkun --------- 24

Home at the café - Gill Ward --------------------- 26

I love you very badly* - Harrison Christian ------ 27

Icarus, plural - Elizabeth Morton ---------------- 28

kia kotahi mai - Piet Nieuwland ------------------ 29

Ko Aotearoa tenei* - Piet Nieuwland -------------- 31

Little God* - Madison O'Dwyer -------------------- 32

Madeline in the mirror - Keith Nunes ------------- 33

may no disaster escape* - Raewyn Alexander ------- 34

Musings of Moonwrecked Angels - Lea Ruth Fernandez 35

Net* - Jillian Sullivan ------------------------- 36

Night Walk - Bradley Nielsen --------------------- 37

Of Dogs and men - John Irvine -------------------- 38

On meeting someone I once understood - Luke Sole - 39

On the way from the ATM* - Jon Little ------------ 40

Paintin a dreamin trail - Maris O'Rourke --------- 41

Play and giggle -Cecelia Fitzgerald -------------- 42

Pretence - Sarah Penwarden ----------------------- 43

Reaching the destination first - Karen Taylor ---- 44

Rejection - Zackhie Bara-Comolli ----------------- 45

Saboor gets an Education - Heather McQuillan ----- 46

Society - Tulia Gonzalez-Flores ------------------ 47

Substratum - Jillian Sullivan ------------------- 47

The mad ones* - Tulia Gonzalez-Flores ------------ 48

The Merry Andrew - Madison O'Dwyer --------------- 49

The Nothing Man - Daniel .E. Hemme --------------- 50

The Question - Luz Saviñón ----------------------- 51

The Sisyphus Thing - John Irvine ----------------- 52

The Totara Calls Absence - Janet Newman ---------- 53

To Old School Friends - Wes Lee ------------------ 53

Two Cities Sophie Procter ------------------------ 54

We Sophie Procter -------------------------------- 55

Wednesday Morning - Sarra Harvey ----------------- 56

White Flowers - Jillian Sullivan ----------------- 58

Words - Fiona Mogridge --------------------------- 58

WE Society Bio ----------------------------------- 59

Editors Note:

Mrs. Thatcher once declared, at the height of her attack on the British Social Welfare System, once the envy of the world: "Who is society? There is no such thing! People look to themselves first."

What Thatcher actually meant by this challenge to the very name "society" was (as she proceeded to explain) the fact that: "Life is a reciprocal business, and people have got the entitlements too much in mind without the obligations."

There is, of course, a lot of truth in this. But that doesn't mean that there are not certain responsibilities on the individual which transcend simple self-interest. The get-rich-quick beneficiaries of Thatcher's new order may have done very nicely for themselves, but all those corporate raids and deregulated industries have left behind a bitter legacy of devastated communities – crime, drug addiction, social and political apathy.

I tried very hard, however, not to impose what *I* feel about society, and its complex relation to the individual, before reading the entries for the "We Society" Poetry Competition. I didn't want to be only looking for poems I agreed with already.

Sure enough, I was astonished by the range of responses and interpretations to the idea of a society of mutual dependence. Some poets took the competition rubric quite literally, carefully inserting the words "we society" – or some variation thereon – in the body of their poem. Others took a more oblique, nuanced approach. These latter tended to be more successful, I think, but both trends are well represented here.

It was very difficult to make a selection from so many good poems: almost all of the writers who entered seem to have fielded their A-team for the competition, but I was eventually able to come up with a longlist of 70-odd poems (all included in this publication), which I then refined further into a shortlist of twelve. Here is that list (in alphabetical order of title):

1. 10 in a packet
A very accomplished, simple but not-so-simple poem about children growing into adulthood, and the things they leave behind, all achieved without fuss or straining for effect.

2. Caring
This is a political poem – almost a manifesto – but it seems to me to personalise its message very effectively: the form is innovative and the language lively.

3. Everything about us
I have to say that I'm particularly fond of the short prose poem as a genre, and there were some very good ones among the entries for the competition. This one was a standout, though – intensely timely, and expressed exactly.

4. Farm
This poem pleased me a lot. As a city-dweller, I share few of the experiences described in it, but the poet made me feel them from the inside. It struck me as a thoroughly *imagined* piece of writing.

5. From me in Vanilla
I like the (disarming) simplicity of this a lot. There were a number of poems along such familiar utopian lines, but this one hinted most successfully at hidden depths below the "new society."

6. I love you very badly
A wonderfully terse, very modern poem, but with ancient resonances to it. The poet formatted it in the tiniest of tiny fonts, but when I blew it up large enough to be visible to my middle-aged eyes, I was quite enchanted by what I read, and its adroit combination of text language and classical love lyric.

7. Ko Aotearoa tenei
The linguistic exuberance and multi-cultural inventiveness of this poem is intoxicating. I must confess that I'd like to read a lot more by this author: this is a dazzling piece of work.

8.   **Little God**
A very intense poem from (I would guess) a very dark place. Once again, what better way is there out of such places than to try and describe it for other people? It can't hurt, and it often helps.

9.   **may no disaster escape destruction in our bundle of sticks on fire**
There's a Neruda-esque delight in metaphor and the long line here: a kind of natural surrealism which brings this old language to life – a rich, complex poem.

10.   **On the way from the ATM**
This is the classic New Zealand storyteller's voice: a well-told tale, almost anecdotal in its simplicity, which draws you in through narrative then forces you to confront uncomfortable truths. Again, the simplicity of it masks the true accomplishment of such a poem.

11.   **Net**
A complex set of associations and memories adding up to a really beautiful piece, one which repays reading and re-reading. This is one of the richest responses to the theme of the competition, I think.

12.   **The mad ones**
I really like this poem. The approach is not unfamiliar ("We are the music-makers, we are the dreamers of dreams" might be seen as a precedent), but there's a charming directness about these "mad ones," and I particularly admire that touch at the end: "So nameless they will write you / A poem / And forget the signature at the end."

Dr Jack Ross works as a Senior Lecturer in Creative Writing at Massey University's Auckland Campus. His latest book *A Clearer View of the Hinterland: Poems and Sequences 1981-2014*, appeared in 2014 from HeadworX in Wellington. His other publications include four full-length poetry collections, three novels, and three volumes of short fiction. He has also edited a number of books and literary magazines, including (from 2014) *Poetry NZ*. Details of these and other publications are available on his blog *The Imaginary Museum* [http://mairangibay.blogspot.com/].

10 in a Packet

Crayon voices
call from the driveway
but before I can locate their whereabouts
they scoot off, leaving only a waxy residue
on the asphalt.

When it rains
you can see the outlines
of children who have grown
out of their skins.

A Picture Paints Words

It's the summer holidays
Kiwis hit the road
head to bach, crib or campsite

Returning Tolstoy to the library
a different holiday picture kerb-side
A van has camped overnight
Driver tidies its contents on footpath

As much distance as can be mustered from the van
dog lies stoned in the middle of the road
Down and out air of *I'm fed up with this and it's the new year*
An unexpected car, and driver lifts longed-for dead-weight clear

On yoga mat joint between lips
another does his morning stretch
Breathes in hallucinatory air and view
of seaside pohutukawa
at location other than this

Tolstoy and I step around the mat

They don't have means for bach, crib or campsite but
bugger it, it's the summer holidays, they're going to have one
The remaining two (she outnumbered) huddle together up front
look more miserable than the dog

Too much weed. No money. This van. Us.

    A Tool

Joining others,
through our commonalities,
finding people
from all over the world.
This once blocked
by our voice,
our tongue,
but now we have a solution.

A tool that changes
the way we see
for better
or for worse
disputable both ways
love it
or hate it...
The internet.

Accent

amidst our bags,
stamped passports
and civil smiles
my grandmother said
to never forget my roots

my black-haired,
respectful,
rosary-clutching roots
to never forget that
I trill my r's

I became a tenant of
the modern man's haven
I got to know their atheists
and their free condoms
I dyed my hair red recently

slowly I will forget
my language
I will adapt to their ways
I will copy their vowels
I will dub dinner as tea

we sometimes call
our grandmother
she's still old
I speak with an
accent now

Amnesia

They tell us dogs chased seagulls along the beaches.
We tell them they exaggerate, the old ones.

They tell us about the smell of mown grass
but we are sick of hearing.

They tell us children swam in rivers.
We tell them they are dreaming.

They tell us they can hear the sound of the ocean.
We tell them their ears are ringing with age.

They tell us they walked outside without masks.
We tell them it is time to go in.

They tell us the rain was like heartbeats.
We tell them to brush off their shoes and their hands.

They tell us there were butterflies and bees in the gardens.
We tell them not to lie in front of the children.

They hum a song about a blue-finned fish.
We tell them to finish their soy curd soup.

They tell us the night sky was lit with stars.
We tell them to put out their lights.

They tell us trees were as tall as silos.
We tell them everything looks big when you're young.

They tell us forest came down to the coast.
We tell them nothing is ever the same.

They tell us tuis flocked in thousands.
We tell them dreams seem real over time.

They jangle their air beads in anger.
We tell them lie still while we breathe.

Amsterdam

The dancing houses lean left
and right. High in a gabled window
a tall boat dreams of
Batavia, its sails of linen
strain to catch the wind,
the smell of cinnamon, the lure
of the Indies.

Threes Xs memories of
fears: water, fire, disease,
build walls on sand to protect
from floods, the night watchmen
to protect from fire, for plague
no cure.

Corpulent burghers with wide
silk sashes, self-satisfied smiles,
bodies corporate. The girls
from eastern Europe once
full of hope, packaged and merchandized,
shop windows shine with Christmas lights
and neon notices warn of bad
heroin and tourist deaths.

Anthropology of Simia

Wind howls.

At the door, who?
> The aged bachelor, red in face, two puffy bags twined.
> A symmetry of size doubled at each side.

He bound, where?
> To the staple of good fortune, the sea.

What, his solace –
> The empty ground.

> "it's a boy," he said.

the first birth since the vessel arrived. a swallow's own.
a dried lantern cherry out the door, charcoals & peppers
> plaited into straw.

> whistle whip through, like undergarment –
> salt-washed white, guts of fishes, open.
> steps branding – crackles of shells, coal-hot sand.

Now I speak your language, but when I was younger, a man approached me with the gurgle. a shot of whistle, a shot of how, a flick og string and stone-beating, *liklhwuuryur.* In truth I thought you would tear me down. A song torn from psalm, the chatter of sea-sunken people.

> grey matter, like veins through
> innards – soft & silky beats, swallowed &the tides
> came in series, hurrying – vying, to a
> better view – at passive, dragging heels.

Each day their hut crumbles a little with the cliff. The consulate pair are stiff with glory of the crown. Wild, their child, made a clay of a skull, and pink plasters water in the dun. A row of translucent peals for teeth, one for each joint of her mother, and a ring of red-paint runny round, muck-slapped brow. A sick child. Her mouth covers the horse's ground.

>   five grubs sprouting – from a flat
>   wound, pooled rain; a shade of hair strung
>   with flower,
>   dapper, a whiplash of winded-down
>   branch, sickly mix of words.

The mother recoils like, beaming down as would like at a dog; "What's it saying, dear?" The professor, at the amphitheatre of market-ring – "Parliament, ecclesia, heliaia, intuitions, functions, ceremonies of rites." Peddler women sit on their bums, a string of eggs sheathed on their laps, toothless at hens pecking at their toes.

>   the old woman, the hill – crooked
>   spines strut under leather – knobbed knees
>   tuck in the road as it falls; tugging a
>   fold at an arm's length by her waist, wound.

At the Bay

a taut azure stretched
behind those clouds
with particular names
cirrus (curl of hair) stratus (layer)
and the fair weather cumulus and
three figures from fifty four years back
grinning and stunned at the length
and breadth of the space between
those days and this one, three different selves
now, age withering them in diverse ways
and directions and what age had not waned

they had somehow done for themselves.
The small magic city across the harbour
blinking them a sparkle of the old dream.

One bending to chat with the local fishers
saying sixty years ago that rock was best
or that tide, or what we caught here.

The other living back his childhood
the concrete roads, the busses, the quiet streets.

And what about the woman?
She was eighteen again taking
that wild exhilarated flight along
the whole distance of the wharf
an abandoned terrifying fling into the harbour.

It looked so far – how had she dared?
And the young poet, so dead now,
so quietened, dashing after her
and next his rough jeans wet
against her legs salt lips kissing hers
it had seemed a triumphant, defining moment.

Then it was a new century and she looked
at those two old blokes and wondered
If I fell in would they even try to save me?

But that night alone
on her own deck, a small slap
in the phosphorescent waves
and an ostentatious full moon
claiming her she smiled and thought

maybe they would.

Caring

I couldn't take it.

I stopped reading about terrorists.
I stopped fretting about conflicts.
I stopped reacting to genocides.
I stopped listening to the fracking.
I stopped watching the extinction of species.
I stopped feeling global warming.
I stopped tasting GE manipulations.
I stopped smelling polluted water.

I didn't want to know.

It won't happen in my lifetime I rationalised until the Ides of March when a baby water dragon roared into my life bringing a new timeline to the back fence, chopped out a hole, filled it with a gate and opened it like a tardis – catapulting me one hundred years forward with free rein to fear his uncertain future of speed, greed, holy jihads.

Now I care.

Confessions

of a bag-lady:
I'm given to looking deep
into my bottle
and seeing the meniscus
there. I reflect on it
though I dread the spiders
that sometimes skitter on its surface

of a postman:
a lifeline unravelling
where once they meant the
thank you postie
now it's Facebook   Skype,
and that spam of spam
email   e-waste
soon no more will dogs
bark at their gates

of a kid:
today I found a worm
it was squirming there
on the cold wet footpath
where there's lots of feet
and so I picked it up
and am keeping it warm
in my pocket
ready for news

of a young mum:
anticipated joy
skin on skin
the bond of breastfeeding
shattered by
this crushing hopelessness
not blues, but blacks

of a poet:
indulgence or a drug
my secret pleasure
and if some poor soul
finds solace there
all the better

date night

she takes her hat off but he leaves his on - the beginnings of an argument, she wants something covering her stretch marks but he demands complete nudity, they are mutually adhesive until she pleads with God and he knows he can let go, cleanliness follows as they try to remember each other's names, she sees him as a strong possiblity so long as he doesn't try to fiddle with her stunning but vulnerable daughters, he has a story to tell his friends - they live through him, they are stuck in army hospital beds waiting for his colourful dispatches, she sees him to the door and passes a phone number, he asks her: "How old are your daughters?"

Digital Natives

These strange creatures
rulers of virtual realms
they are
builders of unseen silos
weavers of fibre-optic messages.

Their native tongue is hypertext
their footprints can be traced
but they never leave an imprint
their traditions are encoded.

Some speak in hyreglyphs
they're characters
bigboy29 speaks and it's all over.

We are strangers
in our own cities.

Pass me the urban dictionary.

Are they training for the craft of war

a world of objects
waiting to be shot down
in the name of a new frontier?

Or do they tell themselves
it's all in their minds?

Engaging with Goya

I : Resolve

It is the year of the brute*. The bull paws the ground,
throwing up dust to muddy the air, money plated and weighed down with
ignorance and megalomania.

The animal bellows and snorts.
Reason stands aloof, spear of knowledge and wisdom
at the ready.

Stiffened by reality she suffers the showdown,
waiting the moment of
right and resolution.

II : Bullying

Welcome to the school for wealthy boys.
Pupils in positions of power terrorise the young and the vulnerable
in 'hazing' rituals.**

Boys made to act as 'prisoners of war', blinded with pillowcases,
led out in the night, physical violence, and
screams of fear.

Rituals and rules in private school and in the wider market place.
Abuse of privilege and power,
intimidation and hypocrisy.

    III : Los Caprichos/Caprices

The seven deadly sins,
greed, gluttony, sloth and lust,
envy, pride and wrath,

as the Catholic Catechism has it.
The selfish placing of the 'I'
above the wellbeing of the 'other'.

The subjective reigning over the objective,
destroying what is vital both to the between,
and the within.

* 'Make way for the Bulls'. From a Goya exhibition at the Auckland Art Gallery, called 'Folly and War', September 2014 – February 2015.

** Event reported in New Zealand Herald, occurring at the elite Auckland King's College private school, October 28, 2014.

Enlightenment

To those seeking
enlightenment
eastern mystics suggest
chopping wood
and carrying water

And then
from the moment
of Nirvana
much the same.

Here, the powers-that-be
point out higher education
as the way forward

Get the marks they say
to make your way
before logging on
three years later
to seek – the hire path

Only now
carrying debt
and sipping
bottled water.

Enough

two dollars eighty
that's enough
for a toilet roll and a small milk
is it?
enough for my four kids
that man in blue
says he got the unemployment down the furthest than any of the others
yet he got no one jobs
he recons the economy is doing good
yet this is the poorest me and my whanau have ever been
now,......how does he work that one out?
I tell you how
One eye on his mate's stripes thinks he's a star,
Other eye should be on the people, but its closed
he makes us wait, then takes heaps, and gives f all
Makes us hungry like America
While he's never had to pinch, sitting in his parlor counting false virtue
He doesn't know us, know what woman have to do,
For our kids
And all my foremothers
and I, got to whore my arse to my man
like some Remuera prostitute masquerading as a kept woman
only, I just get milk and toilet paper
not diamonds and champagne
though I know I've got something more to offer
something more than this
of value, deep down I know it,
But not today
while I'm scraping for red pennies,
And wondering whether it's gonna be bread, or milk we're gonna have
oh well, fuck the excuses
I guess I just ran out of milk

Everything about us

Everything about us makes us strangers here. Out of place tourists waking into another Ramadan day. Into a culture we are privy to but not part of. A neighbourhood free from souvenirs, from brochures and itineraries. The taxi driver asks *Why* ? The memory making of everyday living elsewhere is a blueprint for home. The call to prayer echoes across tiled rooftops, dipping and rising through alleys and stairwells. Our hosts invite us to celebrate Eid al-Fitr: the sugar feast, the sweet festival. But this morning and for seven days more their first meal of the day must be eaten before sunrise, sate them until sunset. We buy street food from vendors who smile at us curiously. Our cameras become dangerous pets questioning intent; tourists bring back photos, travellers bring back stories. But labels are blankets we hide under, revealing selective truths by torchlight. Empty beer bottles replicate like drones on the laminate bench top, then stop. We moderate. Abstain. Our bodies thank us. A new ethos sidles up to the old one, we let parts of it in – no more or less than we need. Children signal our unbelonging in hand-cupped whispers. The mosque's blue domed minaret, zigzagged with gold is striking as lightning in a cloudless sky. Motorbikes and pedestrians move in practiced, haphazard synchronicity, suggesting accidents happen anyway, anywhere. Hijabs form part of the landscape - their colours and patterns individual as dreams. A woman and child cross the road slowly, a small sway over their journey's end. As she bends to his level, the traffic adjusts itself around them. She kisses his left cheek, right cheek, then again – before watching him disappear through the school gates. And this is the familiar. The anchor I hold to. This gesture of loving separation. This unified prayer that all we see in our children will be seen. As we hand them over. As we let them go.

Farm

We slept in the barn.
Pinholes through corrugated iron filled my eyes,
shot darts in the morning;
a thousand lightsabers coming in to wake,
the dog already awake
and the ghost of the boar who twenty years ago
crept in, surprised you beside the open fire.
Where my books mildewed
and I heard everything.
The dog sitting bolt upright,
and stirring. The Upanishads foxed
on the rough concrete floor you painted
American Barn Red.
Now I have to really dig for her name –
the suckling, the Grey Lynn couple won at the fair:
she grew so large, you took her off their hands,
kept your promise she would not be made
into ham hocks and bacon. She only escaped
once – got stuck in the mud of the stream
to the east of the farm.
The dog died in his sleep five years
after I left,
his nose bedded
to his hot belly where the kitten had once
curled.

In my heart a cockerel crows.

fish of the sun

'fish of the sun'
teeming in shoals
afloat on that tide
under sun
'fish of the sun'
that's what i
call it, you know,
just that silver breaking
with shadows on the
tide under sun
swinging, drifting
shoals of them
shining as if
out of a darkness
we don't even
know, always a
time of plenty
among them
but they won't
fatten you won't
fill your hunger
like kumara fish
shellfish or pigeon
there were others
here once who swore,
loved to the hilt, shared
heart amongst them
enough for a whole
people teeming with
talk, poem and song
gone in that silver out
there, just like that,
gone and we here

soon to be gone like
fish of the sun
in blind teeming.

                Te Naupata (musick point), howick

                9 march 2013

from me in Vanilla

I do not need
money in Vanilla
no-one has ever
heard of or used money
there are no banks
or ATM machines
there is no money
living on streets
in Vanilla people
work for nothing

Glittering Towers

I walk through a strange place.
Full of glittering towers.
Broken beggars at their base,
Invisible to corporate powers.
I numbly watch the news.
Try to fathom what we're not told.
We are encouraged to have a view,
Yet silenced when we're too bold.
We are instructed to live lives,

A structured ignorant breed.
True heroes are victimized,
And bigots are rewarded for greed.
It truly is a golden age,
Where money can buy innocence.
And fighters are thrown in a cage,
To wallow in impotence.
If we are to be honestly measured.
Lacking is what we will be found.
For if once we were treasured.
Our self-destruction will astound.
Who will deny that human nature,
Divides between the weak and strong?
Why is it decided by culture,
Where we each belong?
We live in a world ruled by vanity.
So focused on how we are perceived.
That I would question our sanity,
That we don't know we're deceived.
Realize that we are taught lies.
History is written by the victorious.
If we could learn to see through our eyes.
Human kind could be truly glorious.
Time to break down our glittering towers.
Make our beggars our brothers.
Come back to earth's true powers.
Like wayward children to our mother

Haiku

--passing seasons

passing seasons
rubbish blows down the street
I wait to cross

--empty streets

empty streets
the stray dog plays
Marco Polo

--get well

get well flowers
the charity of strangers
needed for more

Heirlooms less abundant

This is what I most want: days
to lean on what is left, and reading
novels thick, and skating
winded on the prow.

Swish my ankles cooling in the
un-hell-loosened breakers, keeping
up a steady stream of now, *not
now, relax, not yet, not now.*

Brush my well skimmed shoes on flat
grey tarmac. Picture self with
thin arms swinging, wearing
heavy boots and jet black farmer's

singlet. Empty sporting venues, grid
lines bright, but ill and fluid under-
neath - because the textbooks say
so, for a few more years still. Sound the

siren - parent ship attempts to leave the
wharf, sport-drink-ridden, dried
fruit curling in my hands and baggage-less,
let muslin wraps flap free, not burdened
down with nappy bags and massage soles and
pushing prams the whole way into town. Not
my journey this time, friend of mine who
purchased all remaining homespun on
the resource kit's behalf is going on the wheel
herself, another round. I shared with her some
snippets of this poem, unsure if she'll hold them
tight or be too busy being, as she's deftly
prone to be, while deftly prone she makes it stanzas

three, and if this were a fairy story, seismic
forces would arise benevolent and give us
more rhyme, shore up sure time, let
another hobby filter down.

Home @ The Cafe

I have become very fond
of this place.
They surely make you
feel at home
... they're friendly always
ready with a smile
and a word
treat you like family.

In fact it's just the place to
 go on a cold day you can
 save on the electric
or read the paper or mags.
I feel as if I could live here
- truly, like for the whole, rest,
of my entire life,

You know anything goes there.
They tell you so
"anything for you
my dear,' they say.
So tomorrow I will be taking in
 my ironing board
and my iron and basket of washing.
A good idea. I'll have company
while I iron and it will be warm.

Should've thought of it sooner

I love you very badly

wet leaves on the asphalt like
garbage and
a smell of rain departing, bro
**
i used to think the crematorium was where creams are made
and the layer of grey particles on our house
was cream dust
**
there are exactly one million cicadas in my backyard
some of them are mating and some of them are dead
**
i am playing GTA vice city on my iPad
i am buying scented candles from kmart at 11pm
**
i am the blueberry kush of the arts
**
you are falling asleep before i can say
i love you very badly
and my hand is falling
into the small of your back
and i am not saying anything
and neither are you
**
listen
that's the sound of
new zealand's quietest heat pump
**
do u remember those underwater castle kits in the 90s
where u had to build a sandcastle in a bowl of water with colored sand?
writing poems is like that
and if poetry is dead i am the embalming fluid
**
barb
**
*brb

Icarus, plural

Ready or not, we fell into the quadrangular
sprawl of suburbs – allotments stiff against
brickwork, cemeteries haunted by spiderwort,
lichen-lit alleyways, wicker furniture, chimneys
and chimneys and disconsolate gnomes.

Ready or not, we fell soft as sparrows,
bled lightly on the tarseal, made pals with chalk outlines,
lay gutterside listening to children's voices
rising from the netball courts. ambulances
hee-hawed along the tree-lined avenues.

Ready or not, we found our legs inside
the hospitals, donned green gowns and
foppish scarves, took to chapels and boarding houses
with maladies robust as sin. we tallied
our blessings on the dormitory walls.

Ready or not, we fell into the laps of our mothers,
bottlefed news-feeds, hot-dogs, soft-core war.
we mimicked asymmetry, played out soap-operas
and infomercials, coddled by emoticons
and the cool speech of Siri.

Ready or not, we learned the alphabets of
our captors, swallowed pills to quench our sentiment,
kicked down lego towers and burned human
paperchains. we blacked-out in ale-houses,
chain-smoked the ashes of our fathers.

Ready or not, we fell for the sight of blunt wings
in the junkyard mirror. we fell for Avon ladies,
pyramid schemes, the brute economics of
ruddy-faced parliamentarians. only sometimes

we looked to the sun.

Yes, ready or not, we found our kingdoms
submerged in a century of polymers. we lay
wreaths atop the power-pylons, tabulated
carbon credits, spent our love on pokies
and postcards of other people's planets.

Ready or not, here we come.

Kia kotahi mai

Kia kotahi mai ki te ao nei *Be as ONE with the Universe*

Through a sky powdered with stars
The voltage of the universe flows
In a permeable magnetic flux

In the vast altar at Moturiki
With medallions of swinging nebula
Gravity is bodies reducing entropy

Kia kotahi mai ki te whenua nei *Be as ONE with Mother Earth*

Blazing orange Moehau moons
Watch our earth in rotation
The light is our skin

Along this coastline of rivers
Summer lightning's of moisture and silver
Humic black Wharekohe silt loams and clays

Kia kotahi mai ki te wairere nei *Flow as ONE with the sacred waters*

With eyes as clear as Waireinga,
leaping water on nga kahawai belly

With Chromista at Port Waikato,
The tributaries gather currents of emerald gulps

Kia kotahi mai ki te hauora *Breathe as ONE with the winds*

Trivento, the three winds
Polar, Zonda and Sudestrada
Rotate the stars in Feng-liu flow

Under an enamel sky, cerulean
Waves of air, lungs of cloud, gossamer bundles

Kia kotahi mai nga iwi katoa *Let us be as ONE in conservation*

From Maungatapere magma eruptions of rata,
Fireworks of blue pigeons against azure sky
Toetoe fronds smoking pollen in the breeze

The we generation,
Flocks of schoolgirls on bicycles
Hair tumbling like swarming bees

Patuki tahi nga Manawa e *Let our hearts beat as ONE in unison with Mother Earth*

Through a torrid summer of blackest pleasures
A dark sultry nymph whispers, sings
Fertile mythologies and adjectival lace

Humid showers in kauri canopies
Cascading taraire, kiekie, nikau
An orchestra tamburica and piano salvos, forte

Ko Aotearoa tenei

Ko Aotearoa tenei
It is not the new state of South Sudan
For here the grass is as green as fire
And voluptuous blossoming milkmaids
Populate the lactating land

On this micro-continent Nieuw Zeeland
Magellan storm clouds fertilized by thunder
Paint the liquid day
And Rat ki rani counts the years
With Hine ahu one

From Puyehue-Cordon Calle
Rikiriki mandated by heaven
Ride nga hau e wha vermillion
With Aye ya fjah ala jou ludl
A new stellar grammar

In this our Arab Spring
the bifurcating sword Dhul-Faquar resonates
with night wind blue of the clear note
and hectic brilliances of black diamond eyes
in hyacinthe flow

It is Tamaki Makau Rau
The galaxy of a thousand lovers

Kakariki Rangitoto nashabat kakariki
Ranginui and synapses of electric green
Horizons of the Pacific continental inter-oriental

In Hauraki snaps
Dames + damozels wear corsets as powersuits
Black roses + baklava + burqua
Exotic sapphires of sea and sky
Gabado Xil + Aurora australis
Sailfish Cove + the oasis
Destiny Bay mystae + Al Maha

At Puwera Tauraroa Tangihua
In the pale hours of the cello
And the theorem
A web of platinum cloud
And obsidian black jade
Elegies of forests Vitex lucens
Puriri + puriri + puriri laughing

Little God

Little God,
are you smudged with rain,
do cobalt whispers fluster
at your toes, are there claws
in your waxen fingertips where lion's paw shells
used to splay themselves upon your skin?

Little God,
did your hand slip as you
nailed down the shorelines,
does the sanctuary lamp flicker
as you walk by, would the apostles spoon

have maudlin poetry bobbing merrily
in your alphabet soup?

Little God,
Does the line blur somewhere between
him and her, are your dreams of kingdom come
a slurry of cognac, Little God, was magma
inspired by the fire within, and did you ever
manage to unhook your lungs from the sword
that Jesus swore was a pain in his side,
and did you ever think of us
before your tome of spilt ink
was sent to press,

Little God?

I went insane a million different times
waiting for you

Madeline in the mirror

Madeline's mask is coming off, the flute blows it's own tune beside her wicker chair in the salon in the mainstreet, she looks at the 50-something face in the mirror and remembers the cuts and waves of her first job, standing behind Bruno Lawrence who fancied a meal between her legs, she didn't recognise him and he gave up, there were dozens of eager young men who paid for a drink and kissed her hand and slipped off the condom at the last minute, Madeline lived among unforecast storms and billowing plastic charmers, absorbing and then later, creating canvasses full of blown-glass light that enveloped, "did it burn?" echoes around a head streaming grey, "I shifted the scars onto the art", and she lets the girl wash her hair and this time, "we'll have it short"

may no disaster escape destruction in our bundle of sticks on fire

anything could appear as a sign in the ashes
a kowhai flower generator for free money and lemon drinks
fun fur embroidered with meat on the head of the prime minister

step into the truth like a lounge
make me stop thinking my life's in danger
today I turned into a park bench with a few birds about
more and more trees and books and beneficial insect life

building a fortress of clean laundry
and children make huts with blankets and chairs against emotions
however we find memory furniture
on a ghost sofa taking each other through home movies

glimpses and recall scans and albums
a double screen sometimes somewhat overlapping
but may we never try to merge and turn bitter with invasion

coming to terms with each intelligence
negotiating around each other's eclectic museum
next keeps appearing fresh and even nonsensical
something unspoken in glances towards choices
do we make things more difficult to see what our limits are?
or is this an accidental trial like with storms or illness?

what could break if we opened the wrong door too quickly?
would that matter – perhaps we'd laugh?
"Careful careful careful," the china ornaments whisper to the cat

Musings of Moonwrecked Angels trapped on Earth Disguised as You and Me

This instance
A mirror of another.
In our expanding universe we can never occupy
An exact space in another time.
So we take photographs and store memories.

Earth Bound
We are but souls and ghosts
Loitering in and littering the planet.
Multi-exposed moments will culminate in a blur
As hours slow down and years speed away.

Wanting to live
All sentenced to die.
We make our chains and pretend to be free.
We judge each other, cast stones,
and in healing forgive.
Pioneer a purpose and hope to be redeemed.

Worship the one true God
Worship the deities.
Listen to the stories of labeled entities.
A blended smoothie of comedy and tragedy--
Imbibed as sustenance for faith and philosophy.

Wanting to live
All sentenced to die.
We are all born to ask why.
When questions are asked answers are sought
but not always found.

How will you fly back home
with broken wings
and both feet on the ground?

Net

The first time I shaved a man
razor and cream,
'attending minutely'
to raspy contours of lip and chin,
his limbs arranged by me in warm water,
he asked *How are you liking your job?*
I said *It's great.*

I've seen the submerged legs of frail patients –
smooth, golden, waxy;
the subterranean skin of those
who no longer stir.

Today, trout trapped
in muddy water after a failed weir.
I held a net in freezing swirl,
their speckled bodies
rose and tumbled.

They, too, gasp and trust
our hands. It comes to this:
some of us
must hold the net,
while some swim deeper.

Night Walk

It is a different quiet in isolation
street lights stack shadows precariously

dew forms atop windscreens
stillness and movement exaggerate in unison

how much of everything is shared
journeys through clusters of sleeping bodies

snake inasmuch as right angles allow
a passing taxi's tyres spread a hush over asphalt

as if the pedestrian were the one to make a noise
and all the while

when the ears must strain
to piece together a faint something

that feels as if it should be music
as if it is

as if it may be music Well
it is a different quiet in isolation

Of Dogs and Men

Give a hound a home, a soft touch,
clean water, treats and his own couch,
he'll love you always
in so many ways
all your days…
he's no slouch.
Give a man a home, a caress,
all your love, your time, nothing less,
wash his 4wheel ute,
love songs on a flute,
tell him he's a beaut,
tell him "Hooray!"
He won't stay.
However much a woman tries,
tempts him with her tremulous thighs,
he'll never agree
about she and he
never be free.
A hound's wise.

On Meeting Someone I Once Understood

The uniform of the dejected and crestfallen,
Faded overalls or tailored shirt and trousers,
You have become an anonymous stranger to me,
You are now indiscernible, unclear,
Your vision and splendour reduced to vacuous pleasantries,
Plywood desk and plastic chair.

You are an image of everyone that inhabits this fractured space,
That have failed to know each other, to recognise themselves in their neighbours and brethren.

It has struck you into obedience, espoused you,
Diminishing sensation and truth,
Our isolation, solitude, grief and pain,
Each more authentic than untruths and banalities,
Is any vocation worth it?

You are angry inside,
I don't blame you,
You once sailed aboard the *Argo*,
You watched over brackish ocean,
Heaving oars combing white-capped mountains.

You are medicated now,
Your gait has stalled to the slowest step,
The Panopticon gaze you triumphed has exceeded metaphor,
An insufferable lightness of spirit.

On the way from the ATM

On the way from the ATM,
after leaving the tended green
campus and crossing Broadway,
a man approaches from out the lot.

The sweltering heat fumes in silence
Up towards the fading sun.
But he wears a striped flannel polo
and a blue sweatshirt tied round his waist.

He pulls a cigarette from his cracked lips, and
shakes his waxed Coca-Cola cup
like a lazy tambourine. The coins clink
out the rhythm of a blues no longer sung.

Your friend strides past, his khaki pants swishing
to the giddy beat of the smooth, paved street.
But you, unaccustomed to the head down rush
of the city, you hesitate.

With stuttering step you rummage through
pockets for spare coins, crumpled bills given
in change. But all you find is a lint tipped pen
and a wallet.

The street light's on the fritz again,
but even in the flickering light you can see
his lips – the black and blue striping,
the cracked skin opening to more cracks.

Your friend turns back with a disparaging grin,
beckoning you on down the street, into the neon night.
In that moment the tambourine shake eclipses
the street's indifferent hum.

From beneath a brow furrowed deep as a field plowed
year after year after year, cloudy eyes rise to meet you.
Caught off guard, you draw your wallet, pull the first bill you touch,
and with a few shuffling steps return to your friend's side.

"You know he's only gonna spend it on booze," he says.
You shrug and smile. You don't want to admit it, but you're happy.

It was only a five.

Painting a Dreamin' Trail to Tennant Creek

Those who lose dreaming are lost
Aboriginal proverb.

They sit in the streets at Tennant Creek
broken glass groups who've lost their way
and sometime lost track of how to seek
any path back to their dreamin' days.

The colonial palettes of Drysdale and Nolan
explode with old and secret terrain
but works by Ngwarray, Kawiny and Burton
unveil different ways to negotiate pain.

A parallel world of indigenous spaces
reveals a new take on traditional ways.
A place of return for the forcibly displaced,
a luminous path to new dreamin' days.

Hope in the colours mapped in the memory
to be carried by Ngak Ngak back to the country.

Play and Giggle

Gone, it seems,

wearing a hat out doors, always
brown smokers fingers
horse and buggy
kerosene lamps
party lines

Now we have

computers and the internet
most things Made in China
sugar addicts by the nation
way too many people
Facebook loneliness

But still

a parent's face is best of all
any relationship can be mended
death brings a brilliant focus
trees live in holy trust
people play & giggle

Pretence

A winter Christmas with
Santa playing saxophone for coins,
and I'm sitting in the warm hush of the tube,
shuffling through stations;
I open my eyes and I'm
still in London.

People are strangely near,
a stranger's leg brushes mine,
fingers touch hands, we sit together
breath-to-breath; I can hear their
sighs, their whispered
conversations;

There's the woman on her phone
announcing in clear, ringing tones:
"You're my fiancé... you're the man
I'm going to marry and you can't
even ring me on my
birthday?"

I pretend not to hear,
but I have entered the hot
fraught space of their lives;
I sit knee-to-knee with the man facing me,
in a blink, he catches my eye,
then looks away.

Reaching the Destination First

Even on the opposite side of the world you are an early person.
Reaching the destination first, you wait,
watching the homeless couple fighting in the park;
confused dogs bark drunkenly around them
and everyone lingering at the bus stop stares
united in an unexpressed pact, the conscious act of non-intervention.

Picking up that thread you unravel the romance,
spin tattered through an eternal city winding up its tougher yarns;
like the two old women camped on a traffic island outside the station,
wrapped in blankets, cooking with coals in a tin bucket,
and when someone nearby says, "Well, they have everything they need,"
you wonder; does that make it a home?

Just around a bend, beyond the ancient bridge
of famous and favoured and photographed angels,
less organised outcasts sleep in the doorways of banks
on the threshold of a chasm, safety in supplicant numbers,
and though you know there's a paradox in there somewhere
your vision is blurred, you can't make the calculation.

Tomorrow there'll be petrol fumes; austerity measuring beggars,
the rate of unemployment up in headlines around the nation,
and you, becoming old, with not a euro to spare, counting the cost
of foreign newspapers you never read beyond the first page,
paying the exchange rate of your relentless new world guilt,
    as Europe begins its rebellion.

Rejection

Open the lock
Come into my house, dragged by the chains of hell
Where whoever enters can never get out
For the doors will slam shut behind them
Tear down the walls, walk down the halls
And step inside my room
I am the one in the corner,
There, but faint, only a shadow
Compared to everyone, everything, consumed in my hate, fear and depression,
Of my own rejection

Saboor Gets an Education

The schoolkids on the bus
fold a map of the world in <u>their</u> heads.
It is marked in mosaic lines
that draw away
from the dust and the biscuit-boy
and sandal straps
that grate harsh against bone-sharp ankles.
His wet tongue presses against the teeth-taste of grit.

His steps are counted,
each a milestone
between car horn blasts.
Each step, a notch
carved with string into his small-boy shoulders.
Each biscuit sold, a coin of little value.
A crack'd drachma.
Desert crumbs.

Each coin is counted,
each sharp elbow-jab,
each beat of the song his mother sang
with flour on her ruby-sunrise arms.

He picks words off a wall, words off a bus,
counts the coins
he carries back to his mother.

The map drawn in <u>his</u> head
is the coordinates
of each speck
of dust on the steep road home
and blasts,
and cold night sky.

Society

A chain of heritage
that changes the shapes
once in a while
when someone
breaks a shackle.

Am I dangerous?

Substratum

We are so vulnerable here.
Our time on earth a time of
how to keep warm and how to be
fed and how to quell our most
anxious thoughts which come back
and back to connection.

How do we stay here on this earth
which is right below our feet?
Soil, clay, substrates of rock,
magma, lava, water, oil, gas;
the things we want to bring up and use,
the things we want to use up.

If all we ever wanted was to know
we would be warm and fed and listened to,
would we be kinder?
Would we in turn listen? Would we understand
the importance of those close to us
and the importance of what is under us?

We have the far sight. And we are what
the shamans warned against.

The mad ones

There is a very peculiar type of being
In this society

Full of beauty that overflows
they cry for nothing
and laugh for nothing

Did I mention that these people
make friends with trees?
and tend to forget names?

They live dreams
without dreaming
for they reality is the best

They open the eyes at night
just to follow that star
that will bring them to dawn

They sometimes forget they have mouth
to speak
so speechless they sing

They sometimes forget they have ears
to hear
so they read the silences
between your words,
the trace of your breath

They sometimes forget they have eyes
to see
so eyeless they admire
your face and the growing of the grass

They have written the many ways
to handless touch a beloved

Those mad ones
tend to forget they have names or stories to tell
So nameless they will write you
A poem
And forget the signature at the end.

THE MERRY ANDREW

Before the war,
I was the leading lady, one leg
Stooped on the chair, the pelt
Of my inner thigh saccharine,
I was classy in fishnet stockings.
Before the war, I had the
wheaten cowlick of your girl next door,
they grasped at my locks, filched off Sif,
they reached for me - their starlet
with the cardinal red pout.

But now,
I know the brain can fluster
Into a nest of white noise, threads
With no ends wrapped around my head,
Now, I know that light is just a lolly
'neath the tongue of night, wasting away,
The spit of me. Now, I am the harlequin,
The hushed head bound in a white net ruff,
And I am the pantomime, and I am the mirth,
And you are the spectators, popcorn
Staling at your feet, tickets on your brow
As if a crown, demanding
    a Merry Andrew

The nothing man

The man with nothing
sits on an empty street;
filled with more nothing
and nothing more.
A man with nearly nothing
sits under the nothing man,
as a cushion of flesh,
as a prayer.
The man with nothing;
now has nothing more,
nothing more
Less nothing.
A man with nearly something
almost salutes;
then sits behind the man
with less than nothing
who now has nearly less nothing.
The man with less than nothing,
chokes a merry tune
sounds of less nothing
and nothing more.
A man with nothing else,
yet crucifix in his throat,
lies still on nothing
in the gutter,
smiling to Jesus,
silent prayer, serves a pillow
for
the man with less than nothing
and nothing else.
Now nothing man smiles
teethless,
with less nothing than before
At the sight of all his-

friends.
As he waits for more nothing,
with a lead pipe, made
of nothing
And nothing more.

THE QUESTION

Dad asked me this morning while we drove if I thought happiness exists, he said *"this holiday season is supposed to be a time for happiness"* but that he didn't see how that was possible. I told him I see a world in crisis, it's inhabitants and it's land going through a crisis, *"amongst this and in spite all of this, brief instances of happiness still exist"* I said. The parents of two little girls walking through the park downtown of a humongous city on a Sunday, visibly from a humble background, they managed to afford public transport and enjoy their stroll and their daughter's giggles. Two sisters going through break ups can support each other and rely on each other's company. Three cleaning ladies giggle in the kitchen on their off-time, preparing a hot beverage and one says *"this is how my grandmother makes it"*. Moments, like seeing two butterflies follow each other in the garden, or seeing someone give their seat to an older person on the bus, lovers embracing in the middle of hundred cars rushing. Keeping a promise of visiting someone on the other side of the world, or sharing a friendly conversation with a stranger in the airport while you share a table and eat. Politeness still exists, sharing with others matters, brotherhood and the common good are bonding links that conduce us to happiness. We must not lose empathy, it's what makes us human, and as humans we shall always continue to pursue happiness.

The Sisyphus Thing

Does nothing ever end
does it go on forever, this toil
this conflict
this unending labour
eternally struggling
to avoid drowning
suffocating
failing continuously
systematically
So why do we persist
in pushing upward
prolonging the inevitable
incessant
unremitting
unrelenting
everlasting
striving for the top
never quite reaching it
Are we are afraid perhaps
success has conditions
requirements
obligations
easier to let the rock go
roll back down
and begin again
bathe in the hurt
bask in the sympathies
O Sisyphus
I understand

The Totara Calls Absence

All AWOL - huia, bush wren, mysterious starling, laughing owl (not laughing now). Strings of a's around the neck of the page. Garroted? No – burned, starved, made homeless, left to die. I? They cut off my arms and legs, carved them into planks. Drove wedges into my sides. Climbed up to my head. Two days it took to saw it off, there were tears all round, my sap ran red. Dragged it to the river by bullock team, floated it on a barge to the mill, came back for another slice off my stump.

Hollowed me out for a bunkhouse. Two of them inside me every night. Then one got a wife!

The fire was hot as hell but it couldn't touch my roots or my bark shell.

Now they gather around with paper and film. I'm a wonder of their world.

To Old School Friends

We heard you were lowered in salt baths,
we heard you were not told about the co-pilot
until you got your strength back.
I saw you years later, one side of your
face untouched, and you still
had that smile: a youngish Robert Redford.
You were the best looking boy.

And the pair on their wedding night
came out in their nightclothes to parade;
an ancient ritual of blessing, of fecundity.
The boy fell down and never rose
the same way. In his pajamas –
these were your days after the wedding.

Two Cities

When the sun shines on my city
glaring
between shadowed alleys
the streets seem dirty.
Every cigarette butt
every piece of gum
shining like rotten jewels
and almost as bright
as black gold
tossed into a paper cup.
Heat rises from melting asphalt
thick and
sticky and
sickly,
echoed by a smokers cough.

But when the rain falls
it cleans the quiet streets.
Scum
succumbs to the
'Slippery When Wet'
and under a canopy of black umbrellas and
vacant eyes
coins don't clink so loud.
My home glistens,
shiny and new like a young ant.
But the face has changed,
character seems gone.
Half of me enjoying a fresh breath
the other
feeling alone.
City sadness is palpable on grey days,
the homeless have tucked themselves away

and I wonder
where do they go in the rain?

We

You can be anyone to someone who doesn't know you.
I could be anyone.
I could be a hundred different people (aren't we all?)
I could be a stone gargoyle keeping a watchful eye over a sleeping city
But cities never sleep
and in the dark the children play, daring one more spin
as they lick sticky sweetness from their lips, tasting
an acidic sting at the back of their throats,
heads dizzy, eyes blurred.
I could be a ghost.
A shadow of a human being
walking through the smokey air - breathe it in!
Breathe me in
I could be dust.
No longer wholly together
yet so unwilling to be torn apart - like Mrs Myers who begged to stay.
But the house had to come down
hazardous! Eyesore!
CONDEMNED.
Memories stacked in every possible place and space - no space!
She lost her cat within the newspapers;
between the boxes of baby clothes and the rotting squash
the cat crawled in and was never seen again,
perhaps uncovering
a hidden portal to another world
where the Mrs Myers of the earth are given magical doors
opening into endless rooms,
where nobody takes you away in an ambulance

disguised as a taxi
to a hospital
disguised as a home.
I could be you.
Walking through these twilight streets,
eyes attached to flickering screens
never to be seen
which means that you don't know.
I could be anyone.
So who are you?

WEDNESDAY MORNING

Break the fast in the morning
with liquid life
just as light is dawning.
The dutiful wife;

check clothes on drying racks.
Grey shadows shrink
and crawl away to hide in cracks
as cloud cheeks turn marshmallow pink.

Slippered soles slide silently,
careful not to mangle the peace.
A saucer fumbled and tumbled violently
like a ripple in time or a sheet with a crease;

the noise is out of place.
A drawn breath.
An intruder in the sacred space. Pause,
silence; you lie in bed like death.

Thoughts percolating and brewing,
chores to choose, jobs to justify.
Ideas from yesterday stewing.
Problems yet to rectify.

A time for stillness and reflection.
That is a luxury one cannot afford.
All done with precision, for perfection,
self-satisfaction is the reward.

Lingering over my cup of coffee
I will the sun to stay asleep,
savouring time like a sweet toffee.
My toast has left crumbs I must sweep.

Eyes flicker to the clock
sitting innocuous and innocent on the chest.
Tick, tock, tick, tock, tick, tock.
Why can't time get tired and rest?

The dishes stare at me accusingly
but your alarm ruptures my world like a shot.
Begrudgingly I make my morning round to your room;
Mother Theresa, Florence Nightingale I am not.

White flowers

If the sun speeds up, like they're telling us,
and the wind plucks at our throats,
 water is the new gold
and food the only uncertainty we crave,
(and shelter)
 then perhaps we'll remember

how we lined the streets, pinned
white flowers
on soldiers marching towards
their life's corruption
while we called hurrah! and our petals
bruised on the road.

Now half of us are marching, propelled
into a future that promises more and
more of power and glory,
and some still pluck and toss the flowers
and some stand like rocks in the maddened flow.
If only enough rocks endure.

Words

Words.
Words are confusing, sweaty and hot,
They're very jumbly when you think of them a lot.
They're like little men that stick in your mind
And paste the alphabet on your inside.
So you remember those jumbled like sounds
That vibrate in your ears when people are around.
Words.

WE Society Bios:

Heather McQuillan writes fiction for children and young adults, flash fiction and poetry. She is a teacher and also tutors with The School for Young Writers in Christchurch.

Tracey Peterson is a student of the the Hagley Writers' Institute, passionate about poetry.
"I am a graduate of Canterbury University having studied English, Linguistics and Education, and am currently working on what I hope will be my first publishable collection of poetry."

E Wen Wong "My biggest poetry accomplishments to date include being published numerous times in NZ Poetry Box, being included in the 2014 and 2015 Rattle Young Poets Anthologies and two poems being published in the Otago Daily Times Extra! Publication."

Sigred Yamit is currently studying Psychology and Linguistics at the University of Canterbury. "I enjoy reading about history, philosophy, art and poetry. My first poem was about crustaceans dancing under the sea."

Janet Newman Her poems have been published in a fine line, bravado, brief, Poetry NZ, snorkel, takahe and New Zealand Poetry Society anthologies. Her essay "Listening Harder: Reticulating Poetic Tradition in Michele Leggott's 'Blue Irises'" is included in the 2015 issue of the Journal of New Zealand Literature.

Jeni Curtis is a member of the Christchurch branch of the International Dickens Fellowship, and editor of their magazine, Dickens Down Under. She has published poems, short prose pieces and short stories in various publications including the Christchurch Press, Takehe, JAAM, the Quick Brown Dog, NZPS anthology 2014, and 4th Floor.

Geum Hye Kim is a cross-over from Korea in New Zealand.

Gill Ward Her poetry, scripts and short stories have appeared in anthologies, magazines, literary publications and on National Radio. Her collection Poetic explanations (Kupu Press) was published in 2011.She won second prize in the 2013 Takahe Short Story Competition and was one of three joint prize winners in the 2013 Printable Reality poetry competition.

Maris O'Rourke has been writing about 7 years and well placed in a number of competitions. Maris's first poetry collection

Singing With Both Throats was published by David Ling Publishing in 2013 to good reviews. She has also had two successful children's books published by Duck Creek Press - Lillibutt's Big Adventure (2012) and Lillibutt's Te Araroa Adventure (2014).

Steve McNeil Husband, father, grandfather, friend, from Orewa. "only in recent years have I discovered my poetic voice. I have lived in New Zealand all my sixty four years, and think I have made a pretty fair contribution to New Zealand society, but have so much more to give."

Keith Nunes was a newspaper sub-editor for more than 20 years but he now writes to stay sane. He's been published around NZ (Landfall, Takahe, Trout, brief, Poetry NZ, Catalyst) and increasingly in the UK and US, was highly commended in the 2014 NZ Poetry Society international poetry competition and is a Pushcart Prize nominee.

Anna Forsyth is a New Zealand poet and singer-songwriter (under the nameGrace Pageant) currently living in Melbourne. Her poems has been featured in Landfall, FourW, Blackmail Press and her debut collection was released in 2013, entitled A Tender Moment Between Strangers.

Dorothy Howie is a researcher on the teaching of thinking in the School of Psychology, at the University of Auckland. Her first book of poetry, called 'Twin Threads' was launched this January, 2015.

Beverly Martens After a successful career in PR and marketing communications, Beverly Martens is now concentrating on her own creative writing. Beverly has had poems published in both the Otago Daily Times and a 'parenting' anthology (despite not having children) unless, of course, you count her delightful, sprightly 14-year-old terrier, Curly.

Vanessa Rare "I have worked in the NZ Film and Television Industry for more than 20 years principally as an Actor and in later years as a Screen Writer and Director. I think I'm most remembered for would be Lead Role in the Feature Film RUBY & RATA, which was shot in 1990."

Jane Williams is an Australian poet and writer. Passionate about travel, she has read her poems at venues in Ireland, England, Canada, Malaysia, Czech Republic and the US. Her most recent book is Days Like These - new and selected poems.
www.janewilliams.wordpress.com

Wes Lee Her chapbook of short stories Cowboy Genes was published by Grist Books at the University of Huddersfield and launched at the Huddersfield Literature Festival in March 2014. She was the 2010 recipient of The BNZ Katherine Mansfield Literary Award.

Peter Le Baige "I returned to Aotearoa in 2012 after an absence of over 20 years and am living an hour's walk from my childhood home. Our family lived 5 minutes' walk from the sea, as my Dad was fond of saying. The water, the tides, the light on water are still everywhere, through whatever I write."

Kerrin P. Sharpe's first book "three days in a wishing well" was published by VUP in 2012. A third collection rabbit rabbit is in progress with a grant from Creative New Zealand.

Anastasia Cook "I am twenty one years of age and Australian born. I've lived in Perth for most of my life but have recently moved to wellington to live with my father who was born here."

Steven Clarkson lives on the shores of Lake Taupo. He is lucky to have the natural surroundings that provide easy inspiration for his work. Steven writes New Zealand based haiku and senryu, little free form poems and prose inspired by nature, people and places particularly Taupo and Raglan.

Janean Cherkun was named Runner Up in the TravCom: New Travel Writer of the Year category in 2014. Janean's poetry is usually inspired by real life events and by the work of her favourite artists, Michelle Evans and Victoria McIntosh.
I love you very badly* - **Harrison Christian**

Elizabeth Morton has a keen interest in neuroscience. In her free time she collects obscure words in supermarket bags. Her own poetry has been published in Poetry NZ,Takahe,JAAM, Blackmail Press, Meniscus and Shot Glass Journal, amongst other places. In 2013 she was winner of the New Voices, Emerging Poets competition.

Piet Nieuwland reads poetry in all sorts of places; arts festivals, beaches, public meetings, libraries, restaurants, hui, art galleries, conferences, hilltops, and bars and cafes and particularly enjoys seeing the response. His self-published limited editions booklets (50-100) often feature a unique picture or design on the cover of each copy.

Madison O'Dwyer has lived in almost all corners of Auckland. She works in dentistry by day, but moonlights as a writer and visual artist. She is a keen observer of people, with a penchant for stepping into other people's shoes and taking a walk.

Raewyn Alexander novelist, prize-winning poet, a reviewer, short story and non- fiction writer. Glam Rock Boyfriends, her third

novel, 2014, is available world-wide on Amazon. Alexander lectures Narrative Writing at UNITEC, and takes other writing classes. Lately she's working on a graphic poetry collection, three pages of which will be in Three Words Anthology, 2015.
www.bookcouncil.org.nz/writers/alexanderraewyn.html
http://poeticjourneytoamerica.blogspot.co.nz/

Lea Ruth Fernandez Nicked "LeaFruit" by friends, she is an asocial freak-of-nature with love for landscapes and quality-alone-time. Through alter-egos named "Aelhtere" & "Bien," she engages in word-plays and off-key crooning ambient in garage sounds, barking dogs, and highway traffic Doppler effects.

Jillian Sullivan has published novels, collections of short stories, a book on mythology, a creative non-fiction book, *A Guide to Creating*, and a poetry collection, *parallel*. Her awards include the Highlights Fiction Award in America and the Kathleen Grattan Prize for poetry. She lives and writes in the Ida Valley, Central Otago, where she is completing her strawbale house.

Bradley Nielsen Originally from Rotorua, Bradley currently lives in Berlin and is studying towards an MA at Freie Universität.

John Irvine lives with his writer/poet wife, whom he met on a Greek island, in Colville on New Zealand's picturesque Coromandel Peninsula in NZ and occasionally lets his dark side out to play with the terrified local sheep. www.cooldragon.co.nz

Luke Sole is a 28-year-old Christchurch-based freelance writer and musician with an interest in New Zealand's political landscape and countercultures. In his spare time he enjoys cycling, tramping and woodworking.. He is currently working on a collection of unpublished short stories and poems.

Jon Little A Tennessee native with a background in hip hop, anthropology and creative writing, "When not working for the rather Orwellian named Ministry of Business, Innovation and Employment, I write poetry."

Cecelia Fitzgerald remembers vividly striding through the Ashburton Domain, not knowing if she would ever be able to live in her home again, if her family would survive, if she could get bread or petrol and a voice booming in her head 'Alright, alright, I will be a writer'. She has published poems in The Press, a fine line, and Flash Frontier.

Sarah Penwarden "I worked as a counsellor for ten years and I am now a counsellor educator. I have had poems published in Poetry New Zealand, Meniscus (AUS), poems and short stories published in Takahe magazine, and a short story broadcast on Radio New Zealand."

Karen Taylor "Creative writing is an important part of my life and I have attended numerous courses and workshops over the years at various institutions, most recently completing a paper at Victoria University."

Zackhie Bara-Comolli "I primarily write songs, stories and poetry, including scriptwriting, also contributing researched and written material to a published writer. My creative ideas are inspired by the extremes that can arise without much warning and have a lasting effect on us, as well as cycles, physical and mental process of how a person might perceive and handle this."

Tulia Gonzalez-Flores "I am nurse specialized in medical research and public health. I arrived in this country sailing a small yacht (31ft) from the cost of Mexico trough the pacific islands and finally arriving here last year. I started a Blog in 2014 about my travels and poems in Spanish."

Daniel .E. Hemme "I am sixteen years old, I live in Auckland and attend Long bay college. I started writing at about 8 years old and have never stopped."

Luz Saviñón is a Mexican born documentary filmmaker interested in themes of social justice and politics. She has made Aotearoa New Zealand her permanent home and works in the local film and tv industry.

Sophie Procter "I work full time as a barista and bar manager at a cafe on Karangahape Rd, although really it's more of an institution. I take part in the Poetry Live open mic nights most Tuesdays at the Thirsty Dog (also on Krd) and have been a featured reader there during their Woman's Night event in 2014."

Sarra Harvey "I am a trained secondary school teacher (English, social studies, history, drama) and am taking this year off to stay at home with Roma. I love instilling this passion in others as well. I fell in love with poetry during high school when we studied Sylvia Plath."

Fiona Mogridge MIB, BCom, ATCL "I'm a passionate performing arts practitioner working in theatre, film and television. Most often as an actor, more recently teaching drama to children - which I just love, it's such a privilege and full of energy and creativity. I wrote the poem 'words' when I was eleven years old and on holiday in the Bay of Islands staying in a caravan with my best friend."

www.ingramcontent.com/pod-product-compliance
Lightning Source LLC
Chambersburg PA
CBHW071414290426
44108CB00014B/1815